THE
MAGNIFICENT
CONTINENT

THE
MAGNIFICENT
CONTINENT

RAND McNALLY & COMPANY
New York Chicago San Francisco
in association with
Mitchell Beazley Publishers Limited, London

The Magnificent Continent was edited and designed
by Mitchell Beazley Publishers Limited
87–89 Shaftesbury Avenue, London W1V 7AD

Editor: Iain Parsons
Art Editor: Pat Gilliland
Assistant Editor: Marsha Lloyd
Designers: Michael Blore, Roger Hammond
Art Assistants: Pauline Faulks, Carol Johnson
Picture Researchers: Ken Kahn, U.S.A.
Kate Parish, Susan Pinkus

Publisher: Bruce Marshall
Art Director: John Bigg
Executive Editor: Glorya Hale

EDITORIAL ADVISORY BOARD
Photographic Adviser: Arthur d'Arazien
Editorial Advisers: Dorothy Millikan, Paul Tiddens
Art Adviser: Ed Day

The Publishers acknowledge the generous
cooperation of International Paper Company,
whose regard for a priceless heritage
helped make this book possible.

ISBN: 528 81011 1
Library of Congress Catalog Card Number: 75-1928
Printed in the U.S.A.

6 INTRODUCTION

8 THE FOUR AGES OF A CONTINENT
Norman Gelb

42 COAST OF WONDERS
Marina Warner

56 NORTHWEST PANORAMA
John Dyson

70 LANDSCAPE OF ETERNITY
John Dyson Christopher Davis

90 MOUNTAIN MAJESTY
John Dyson

108 THE ENDLESS RANGE
John Dyson Norman Gelb

124 LAND BY THE LAKES
Nicholas Harman

138 CONFEDERATION OF CONTRASTS
Nicholas Harman

172 ATLANTICA
Nicholas Harman

204 THE GREAT LAND
Bryan Sage

216 HAWAII
Marina Warner

224 CANADA
Jurek Martin

246 MEXICO
John Julius Norwich

254 THE GAZETTEER OF GREAT PLACES
Richard Dunlop

314 INDEX

INTRODUCTION

This book is dedicated to the grandeur of a continent. It is a tribute to North America—to its soaring mountain spires, its stark mesas and gaping canyons; to its rugged shores, haunting lakes, meandering rivers and thunderous waterfalls; to its proud, brooding forests and formidable deserts; to its magical subterranean caverns and vast undulating plains; to its sprawling cities and backcountry hamlets; to the continent's grandiose spectrum of wonderous sites and aspects.

This book is dedicated to the American dream, in which the lure of the land has always been a central theme, fashioning the character and aspirations of Americans, offering visions of eternity, facets of reality transcending human fragility and a retreat to innocence. This book is, for the most part, an exercise in discovery and rediscovery, a quest for elusive dimensions of beauty and truth, for values untarnished by time but often eroded by neglect. Not without wisdom did the Indians endow North America's natural wonders with mystical spirits to be venerated. Not without reason have so many

of these natural wonders now become natural shrines.

This book is dedicated to the moods and meanings of the North American landscape—to the opaque, tangled serenity of the Okefenokee Swamp; to the tempestuous spasms of the sea crashing endlessly over rugged rock formations of the Oregon shore; to the desolate enchantment of Canada's limpid North Woods lakes; to the craggy majesty of the Grand Tetons; to the dazzling polychrome antiquity of the Petrified Forest; to the bleak volcanic glory of Popocatepetl towering over the Valley of Mexico.

This is an expedition through the vestiges of primeval America, touched and transfigured over inconceivable dimensions of time by titanic elemental forces beyond human influence. But it is also an exploration of North America's overlaid tiers, the works and ways which bear the stamp of mankind.

This book is, therefore, dedicated, too, to the people of North America—to the prehistoric men out of Asia who were the first humans to plant roots on the

continent; to the richly diverse and scattered Indian cultures and civilizations which succeeded them; to those audacious explorers who, seeking other realms, stumbled comparatively recently on America's shores and ultimately realized the enormity of their discovery; and to those who followed them and, through toil and ingenuity, built the brave New World they had expected to find.

During his relatively brief tenure on its soil, man has transformed North America. In the process, he has constructed an imposing physical context of his own upon the bedrock of the land. Although not as durable as that which nature molded, it is an integral element in the image of the continent. This book is, therefore, dedicated to the lofty concrete and glass grand canyons of North America's bustling metropolises as well as to the Grand Canyon of Arizona; to the cactus-like totems of the northwest coast Indians as well as to the elegant southwest desert cacti; to down-to-earth small-town main streets as well as to cloud-obscured mountain passes; to graceful bridges spanning yawning waterways as well as to the rivers that flow down to the sea.

This, then, is an excavation as well as a pilgrimage, focusing on visual substance as well as basic significance. The perspective is new, unjaded, fresh; it is that of writers from other lands who went to North America to examine, to explore and to feel uniquely the uniqueness of the continent's prodigious natural and man-made spectacles. Peaks, prairies, plateaus and plazas, the setting is immense, both in size and concept. The continent's splendors are strewn across it like windblown seed. Nevertheless, there is a fundamental underlying confluence—this is North America; its constituent parts comprise a whole. We have sought here to weave together its various threads, to compile a catalog of distinct, vivid impressions, both descriptive and instinctive, and, from those extractions, to construct an image of a magnificent continent.

THE EDITORS

THE FOUR AGES

OF A CONTINENT

AGE ONE
A Continent is Born

North America has been defined and redefined, discovered and rediscovered, by accident and design, time and time again. It is an illuminating process still unfinished. However, to fix the continent in time and place is an elusive undertaking. Compass readings, statistical tables and this morning's headlines are instructive. But North America's history is a compendium of spectacularly diverse fragments of time, each punctuated by momentous events. Its landscape has been sculptured by a staggering variety of elemental forces and mortal designs. Its mosaic of natural and man-made monuments conveys an infinity of moods—awesome like Death Valley, turbulent like the Colorado River rapids, placid like Canada's Athabasca Glacier, frenetic like downtown New York, luxuriant like the Yucatán jungle, austere like the Dakota Badlands.

The face of North America today is merely the most recent of the many profiles the continent has displayed since the world took shape

9

from a cloud of celestial gas four and a half billion years ago. What happened so long ago is impossible to determine with certainty; the sequence of events, and the events themselves, are disputed by scholars and scientists. One theory of the origin of the continent suggests that the molten globe, into which the earth was transformed as it grew palpable, cooled unevenly; that North America and the other continents solidified first; and that the remaining, still molten areas subsided before hardening to form permanent oceanbed depressions.

Another theory conceives of North America as originally part of a solitary super-continent —called Pangaea—which was molded from the earth's congealing surface. This enormous landmass was subsequently shattered by terrestrial cataclysms into the various continents, which, in a process begun billions of years ago and still continuing, at a rate of one-half inch a year, drifted into the positions they occupy today. Matching contour traces of their continental shelves still show how Northwest Africa may have slotted into North America's eastern seaboard.

Other theories about how North America began have been advanced and no doubt still more will be propounded. But whatever its origins, the continent was at first, and for a long time thereafter, a lifeless landmass in the explosive process of taking form and shape. Volcanic turbulence thrust up towering mountains, capped with smoldering craters, which spewed forth torrents of lava. The continental crust cooled and contracted. It buckled and buckled again, lifting and shifting mountain spines. Earthquakes shattered and rearranged the void. Primeval seas —inhabited by minute marine creatures, the first living things—repeatedly washed across the continent, obliterating the landscape.

Time is a tease when it comes to contemplating these events. A thousand years is a fleeting instant, barely worth mentioning. A million years is a brief moment, leaving the barest of legacies. A half billion years ago most of North America was inundated. Oceanic intrusions advanced and retreated, eroding and leveling the rock outcroppings they drowned. What is now Arizona was once an island ringed by lapping waters. So was most of Oklahoma. The Great Plains were once totally awash—immense submerged lowlands between higher ground east and west. The high ground was eventually lowered and inundated as well.

Some two million square miles of eastern and central Canada remained untouched by the deluge. This Canadian Shield, the continent's most ancient stable-surface rock formation, a vast storehouse of mineral wealth, took shape more than a billion years ago and, as far

as is known, has never since been submerged. A chain of formidable mountains, snaking down from the shield through eastern America to Alabama, also remained largely high and dry, as did isolated peaks and plateaus elsewhere. But, for the most part, the seas came and went as if there were no continent there.

The submerged areas were not left unaltered. They remained subject to geological convulsions, volcanic eruptions, earthquakes and the folding of the earth's surface. These subterranean regions were also relentlessly veneered with thick strata of sediment. Like coffee grounds settling to the bottom of a pot, countless particles of terrestrial and marine debris sank to the floor of the inland seas and, over a long period of time, hardened into layer upon layer of rock, to be raised, lowered, split asunder and worn down by subsequent upheaval and erosion.

Many such uplifted protrusions as the Grand Canyon and Monument Valley buttes and mesas reveal their venerable sedimentary composition in rainbows of rock stripes, one atop the other, which mark their sides—billions of sand particles, which dropped to the beds of ancient seas and petrified into sandstone layers; mud, which was transformed into shale; and limestone formed from enormous masses of compressed marine skeletons and shells. Each layer, each color, signifies a small eternity which mocks our conventional calendars.

Sediment, often many thousands of feet deep, is the primary constituent of North America's topography, as well as the stuff from which much of its scenic beauty has been hewn. Kentucky's Mammoth Cave, the Carlsbad Caverns of New Mexico and virtually all of North America's underground natural cathedrals are carved from limestone laid down by primal inundations and sculptured by erosion after the seas retreated. The haunting natural arches of Utah were fashioned from sandstone, once submerged. Thick layers of shale which lined the bed of the Niagara River were gradually washed away, undermining a cap of more resistant rock; the resulting collapse produced Niagara Falls. Ancient ranges, like the Nemaha Mountains of Kansas, which once were silhouetted against the horizon, but are now only geological footnotes, were lost beneath the floors of prehistoric seas. They were matched, then buried by accumulating sediment.

A warm, moist climate pervaded the continent during the time of the inland seas. Dense thickets of vegetation sprouted in swamps along the rims of the water and in its shallow reaches. Immense forests also sprang up, to be smothered when the seas advanced and to grow anew when the seas contracted. New woods flourished over the remains of the old,

burying their predecessors and buried, in turn, by their successors. Layer upon layer of dead forest was compressed beneath the surface. The result, after time and the earth's chemistry had done their work, was fossil fuel —the rich coal seams of the Appalachians and of Nova Scotia.

The semitropical swamps and marshes ringing the inland waters were an evolutionary incubator. Higher and higher life forms evolved. The waters teemed with fish and mollusks. Amphibians emerged onto the land. Mammal-like reptiles ranged through the jungles and forests in search of sustenance. The most formidable creatures of all, perhaps of all time, were the dinosaurs, grotesquely huge giants, masters of the continent, and of the earth, for more than a hundred million years—far longer than man's tenure so far.

In the swamps of Connecticut and New Mexico, in the primeval jungles of Missouri and Utah, in the steamy marshes of Alberta and North Carolina, enormous, ferocious carnivores and massive, plodding herbivores hulked across the landscape. The skeleton of a brontosaur, which was ninety feet long and weighed an estimated thirty tons, has been reclaimed from a quarry in northwestern Colorado. Excavations among rock beds near Hell Creek, Montana, have uncovered the bones of *Tyrannosaurus rex*, which stood fifty feet tall, had a thirteen-foot stride and a skull four feet deep, the powerful jaws of which were armed with sharp teeth six inches long. Other explorations nearby have produced the battlemarked remains of its mortal enemy, *Triceratops*, an armored behemoth with long, pointed horns above each eye and another over its snout. The duck-billed *Trachadon*, whose elongated mouth contained two thousand teeth, roamed the marshes of western New Jersey.

There were fifty-ton brachiosaurs, so heavy that they lived most of their lives in water to sustain their weight, having evolved nostrils at the tops of their heads so that they could breathe when almost entirely submerged. There were stegosaurs, tank-like creatures with large, protective, bony plates protruding from their backs and long spikes projecting from their tails. Voracious flying dinosaurs, with fifty-foot wingspreads, dominated the skies. Fifty-foot-long marine reptiles, cousins of the dinosaurs, were lords of the depths of the inland seas.

There were also small, bird-like dinosaurs, as well as the earliest of mammals, diminutive animals, including primitive rodents, which sheltered in high ground. But for no reason yet understood, this was an age of giants, of massive beasts who, despite their size, or perhaps because of it, were destined to disappear forever.

THE DRIFT OF A LANDMASS

The earth's original supercontinent, Pangaea, began to break up about two hundred million years ago. About seventy-five million years ago South America and Africa had separated, but North America and Eurasia still formed one landmass known as Laurasia. North America and Greenland broke away about forty-five million years ago and drifted west to their present positions.

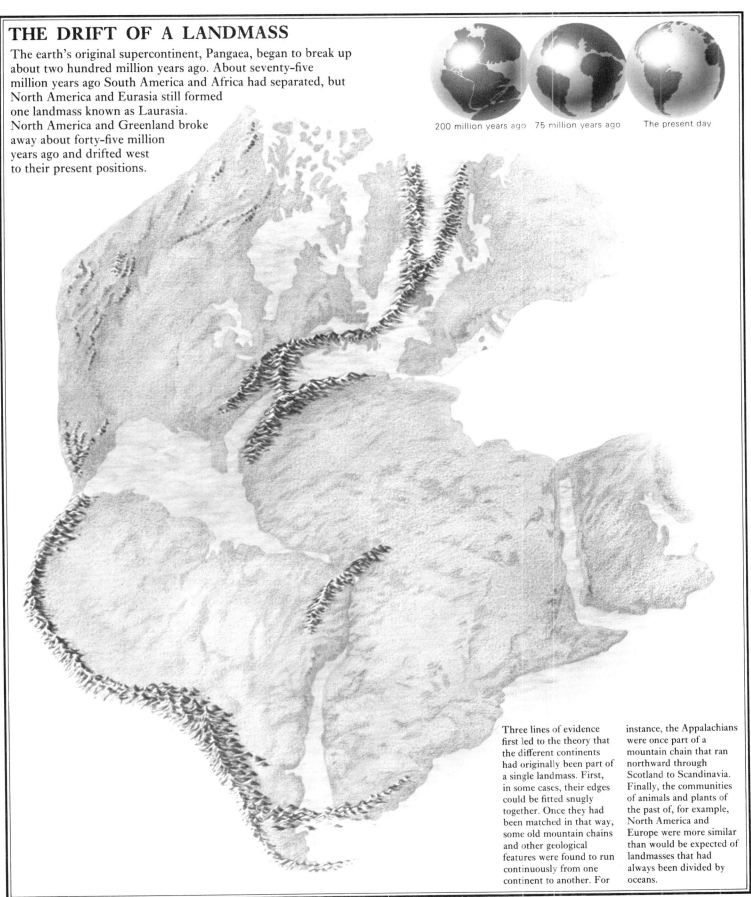

200 million years ago   75 million years ago   The present day

Three lines of evidence first led to the theory that the different continents had originally been part of a single landmass. First, in some cases, their edges could be fitted snugly together. Once they had been matched in that way, some old mountain chains and other geological features were found to run continuously from one continent to another. For instance, the Appalachians were once part of a mountain chain that ran northward through Scotland to Scandinavia. Finally, the communities of animals and plants of the past of, for example, North America and Europe were more similar than would be expected of landmasses that had always been divided by oceans.

NORTH AMERICA IS FORMED

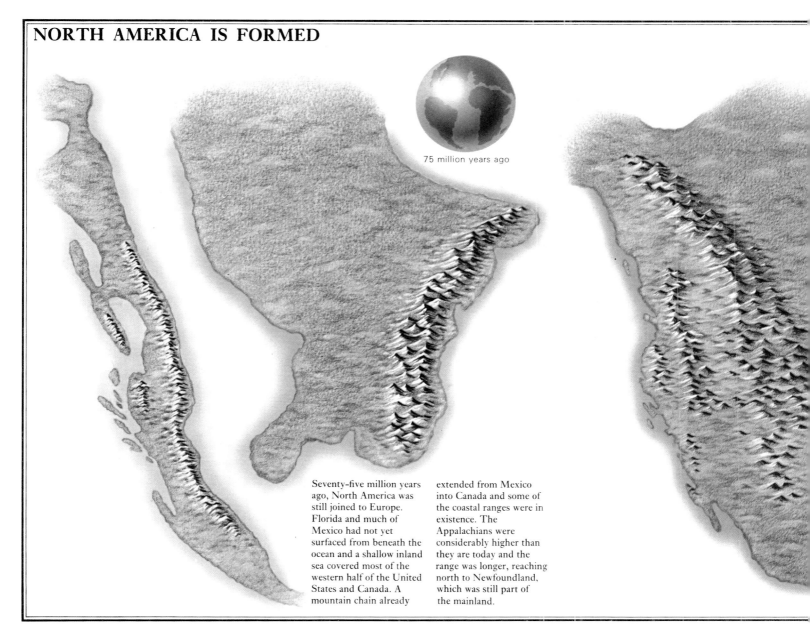

75 million years ago

Seventy-five million years ago, North America was still joined to Europe. Florida and much of Mexico had not yet surfaced from beneath the ocean and a shallow inland sea covered most of the western half of the United States and Canada. A mountain chain already extended from Mexico into Canada and some of the coastal ranges were in existence. The Appalachians were considerably higher than they are today and the range was longer, reaching north to Newfoundland, which was still part of the mainland.

The dinosaurs were probably doomed to extinction by environmental changes. The inland seas slowly withdrew. It grew colder. The swamps and jungles disappeared. Suited only to the conditions in which they had flourished, too ponderous to trudge long distances in search of other subtropical regions, the dinosaurs vanished from the face of the earth.

Their reign was succeeded by long spans of climatic fluctuation. Arid periods turned vast expanses of North America into windswept deserts. There were temperate periods, many millions of years long, during which rainfall wove webs of drainage systems across flatlands and through mountain belts. Wind and water eroded jagged peaks. Enormous forests sprang up, one of which covered most of eastern America. Mammals inherited the

continent from their vanished reptilian forebears—among them were giant horned pigs, elephant-like mastodons with shovel tusks protruding from their lower jaws, *Eohippus*, the dawn horse, barely two feet long, and tiny rhinoceroses, almost as small.

A new period of accelerated subterranean disturbance was initiated. Mexico's central tableland was uplifted, as was much of the southern coastal plain, which rose from the sea, Florida last of all, emerging from watery depths a mere forty-five million years ago. Chains of volcanic eruptions threw up the Columbia Plateau in the Pacific Northwest, as well as mountains in Alaska and California. A plateau was raised in northern Arizona from which the mighty Colorado River was later to carve the Grand Canyon. The Rockies were uplifted from a sediment-filled trough in the

west and rain-fed streams washed sediment from their cloud-brushing heights into lowlands to the east, laying a bed for the Great Plains, a process duplicated in valleys of mountains great and small across North America.

Still another major force was to be unleashed before the continent took the features that are known today. In the Canadian north, vast ice sheets, as thick as ten thousand feet in places, were accumulating. A million years ago—only yesterday in the continent's overall time scale—these glaciers began inching down over North America, advancing up to one foot a day, pushing forward, scraping and grinding down everything in their paths, fundamentally altering the regions they covered. They chiseled canyons and ravines out of plateaus, redirected river beds, smoothed out plains,

THE DRIFT OF A LANDMASS

The earth's original supercontinent, Pangaea, began to break up about two hundred million years ago. About seventy-five million years ago South America and Africa had separated, but North America and Eurasia still formed one landmass known as Laurasia. North America and Greenland broke away about forty-five million years ago and drifted west to their present positions.

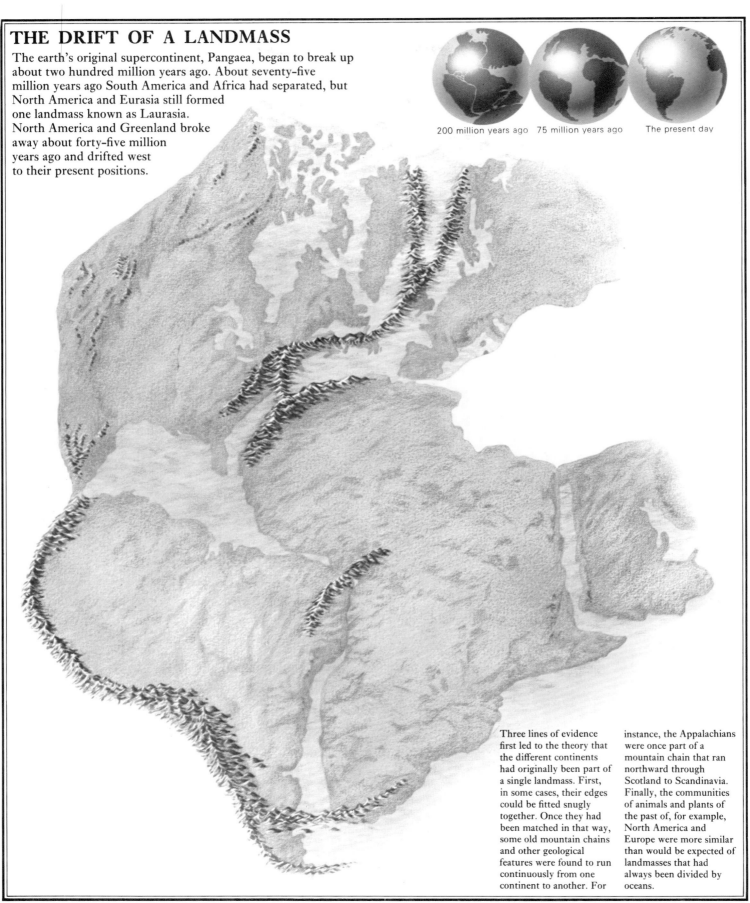

200 million years ago   75 million years ago   The present day

Three lines of evidence first led to the theory that the different continents had originally been part of a single landmass. First, in some cases, their edges could be fitted snugly together. Once they had been matched in that way, some old mountain chains and other geological features were found to run continuously from one continent to another. For instance, the Appalachians were once part of a mountain chain that ran northward through Scotland to Scandinavia. Finally, the communities of animals and plants of the past of, for example, North America and Europe were more similar than would be expected of landmasses that had always been divided by oceans.

11

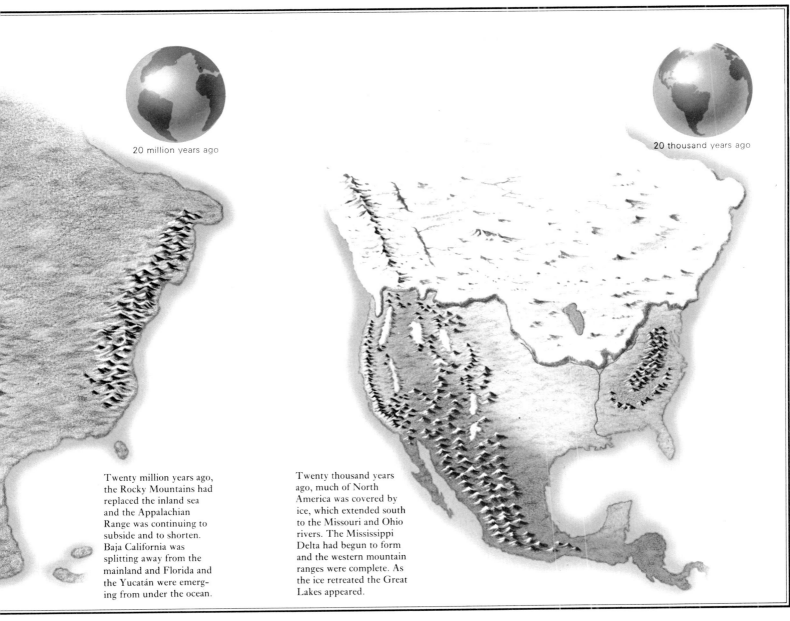

20 million years ago

20 thousand years ago

Twenty million years ago, the Rocky Mountains had replaced the inland sea and the Appalachian Range was continuing to subside and to shorten. Baja California was splitting away from the mainland and Florida and the Yucatán were emerging from under the ocean.

Twenty thousand years ago, much of North America was covered by ice, which extended south to the Missouri and Ohio rivers. The Mississippi Delta had begun to form and the western mountain ranges were complete. As the ice retreated the Great Lakes appeared.

filled in or tore open valleys and pried loose and transplanted huge quantities of soil and stones.

Topsoil was picked up in the north and deposited off the eastern coast to form Cape Cod, Martha's Vineyard and Long Island. California's Yosemite Valley was carved by glacial might. The basins of the Great Lakes and of thousands of lesser lakes were gouged out by the ice walls. Canada, New England and the north were denuded of their rich vegetation and sprawling forests. Tree seeds were carried south by glacial winds to provide the genesis of forests of fir and other northern trees that were to spring up in regions where such trees had never before grown.

There had been earlier glacial periods, lost in obscure recesses of archaic history and geological transformation. But the ice ages

which have left their distinct mark occurred within the last one million years—four major glacial periods and several lesser ice ages during which the glaciers crept relentlessly down across the continent, reaching as far south as a line from what would later be New York to St. Louis, then skirting up and stretching to the Pacific just south of the Canadian–American border.

Frigid temperatures created and propelled the ice walls; a warming process brought them to a halt. Each of the ice ages drew to a close (the last one about ten thousand years ago) as the glaciers slowly melted, releasing huge amounts of water to create new rivers and streams and to widen those which had survived the glacial assault. Some glaciers, smaller and less thick, survived; some still do, including those in Canada's Columbia Icefield,

in Alaska and the remnants of ice sheets clinging to the crags and flanks of Mount Rainier and the Grand Tetons.

North America throbbed to life again during interglacial periods. Warm, sometimes subtropical climates nourished new forests and a resurgence of plant life. Fish teemed in swollen rivers, which surged to the sea to unload their glacier-fed rapids, and in the waters of glacier-carved lake basins. Mammals, including giant sloths, camels and saber-toothed tigers, flourished in highlands and lowlands.

Each return of the glaciers spread a white shroud over the continent's life and activity, creating polar deserts wherever they extended. But it was during one of the great ice ages that the most highly developed mammal of all, *Homo sapiens*, already long resident elsewhere, first discovered America.

AGE TWO
The First Americans

The human species, according to all available evidence, is not native to America. Man did not evolve through successive stages from ape-man to human being on the American continent, as he did on other continents in other parts of the world. The first Americans were full-fledged humans, who migrated from somewhere else. But who they were and where they came from has long been disputed.

It has been claimed that the first people to discover America were survivors of lost continents—explorers or stragglers from Mu, which, it is said, sank beneath the Pacific Ocean thousands of years ago, or of Atlantis which, it is contended, disappeared beneath the depths of the Atlantic before recorded history. Others say the Indians are descendants of the lost tribes of Israel, or of Phoenicians, Greeks, Egyptians or others, who navigated uncharted seas on ancient, perilous, forgotten voyages of discovery. However, the evidence of the first Americans—prehistoric remnants and remains, biological affinity and geological probability—points elsewhere, to northeast Asia. It is now generally accepted that the earliest Americans were nomadic stone age hunters who came from Siberia and who left a paper chase of archaeological clues to their identity and to their line of march.

Today, Siberia and Alaska are separated by a fifty-six-mile-wide breach of comparatively shallow choppy water. But, during the ice ages, glaciers which blanketed much of North America, but not Alaska, imprisoned so much water that the sea level dropped as much as three hundred feet, exposing a broad isthmus of land, a bridge more than a thousand miles wide, which linked America and Asia. Wandering herds of animals—including mastodons, long-horned buffalo and musk oxen—which grazed on the Asian side, casually drifted across this fertile landbridge and into Alaska. The nomadic Siberian hunters, following their prey and extending their range of scavenging for wild edible plants, unwittingly found the American continent, too.

Their discovery of America was unintentional and unperceived, an accident neither recognized nor understood by those involved. The first humans to set foot on the North American continent crossed no noticeable frontier. They overcame no natural barriers, contended with no hazards they had not previously encountered and forsook no permanent home to find a new land.

It is difficult to determine when this happened. There was at least one, and perhaps several, glacial periods during the era of primitive man when the Alaska–Siberia landlink was above sea level and accessible to the nomads out of Asia, whose heirs were, at least for a time, to inherit America. Bone and stone implements several thousand years old, similar to others found in Siberia, have been uncovered in Alaska. Present-day climatic conditions in both those regions complicate the search for such relics. Radiocarbon tests, however, have shown that a human skull found near Del Mar, California, dates back forty-eight thousand years. Remains of what is believed to be a thirty-eight-thousand-year-old charcoal hearth have been found at Lewisville, Texas. Carved bone implements dating back thirty-two thousand years have been discovered at Tule Springs, Nevada. Near Snake River, Idaho, the bones of bison have been uncovered, which show signs of having been killed by hunters thirty thousand years ago.

It may have taken thousands of years for man to make his way down from Alaska to the North American heartland. It is likely, then, that the first crossing from Siberia took place at least fifty thousand years ago, and perhaps earlier. New discoveries—a human bone here, a primitive tool there—keep pushing the date back in time.

It is probable that the first Americans arrived in trickles rather than in waves, an evergrowing procession of small hunting and plant-gathering bands. The migration may have been halted for long periods by the submergence of the landbridge as glaciers melted and may have resumed when a new ice age drew back the sea and again opened the path from Asia to America.

The first Americans are believed to have had prominent cheekbones, slightly slanted eyes, straight black hair and reddish-brown skin. Some anthropologists, however, suggest that the early migrants may have arrived from Asia before the racial characteristics of *Homo sapiens* became sharply differentiated, in which case the ancestors of the Indians would have developed Mongoloid characteristics over a long period of time subsequent to their arrival from Asia. Later arrivals, including the Eskimos—whose ancestors probably first crossed from Siberia about ten thousand years ago—were more distinctly Mongoloid.

With the glaciers relatively close, the winters were fiercely cold. The first Americans probably wore animal skins and furs and built fires. Perpetually on the move, they lived in easily constructed, readily abandoned homes, probably pit shelters covered with animal skins. They traveled in communities that

IN PURSUIT OF BIG GAME

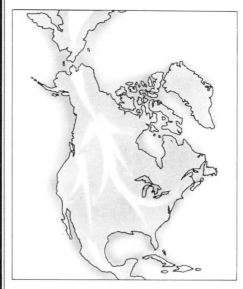

The first Americans came across the landbridge from Siberia about twenty thousand years ago. They were nomadic hunters who pursued the giant mammals which then roamed North America. Their pursuit of game gradually carried them southward, down the east and west sides of the Rocky Mountains, until they eventually reached the Gulf and Atlantic coasts. Some pushed onward into Mexico and South America. The finds of archaeologists show that these early Americans, armed only with stone-tipped spears and rocks, hunted and killed woolly mammoths, which stood nine feet tall, and giant sloths, which, when they reared, were twenty feet tall.

were tightly knit by the need for numbers to subdue the formidable animals on which they preyed. It is unlikely that individual hunters, armed with stone knives and stone-tipped spears, which they launched from spear throwers, could overcome woolly mammoths, which stood twelve feet tall and weighed several tons.

Early man in America was neither an explorer nor an adventurer. No irrepressible urge led him out of Alaska and across the continent. He was lured on by the same impulse that had brought his forebears across the landbridge. He was a hunter and he followed his prey. No doubt some pursued wandering herds—including camels and horses, which were to become extinct in the western hemisphere—back across the landlink to Siberia. (Spanish conquistadors were later to reintroduce horses in America.)

Although the plains and valleys of Alaska were habitable, a barrier of glacial ice blocked

14